I Love Snow Babies

QEB

Camilla de la Bédoyère

Editor: Harriet Stone
Designer: Melissa Alaverdy

Copyright © QEB Publishing 2017

First published in the UK in 2017
by QEB Publishing
Part of The Quarto Group
6 Orchard, Lake Forest, CA 92630

A CIP record for this book is available
from the Library of Congress.

ISBN: 978 1 68297 218 2

Printed in China

FSC
www.fsc.org
MIX
Paper from
responsible sources
FSC® C016973

Picture Credits
fc= front cover, bc=back cover, bg=background, t=top, b=bottom, l=left,
r=right, c=center

Alamy: 5tr © RGB Ventures LLC dba SuperStoc, 6br GROSSEMY VANESSA,
32 © imageBROKER, 33br © Philip Mugridge, 34-35 All Canada Photos, 39b
Thomas Lee, 40tr © Accent Alaska.com, 50 WorldFoto, 51t Cultura RM, 51br
WorldFoto, 56tl © PhotoAlto, 56b © WILDLIFE GmbH, 57bl © Eric Isselée,
57br © GROSSEMY VANESSA, 75t © Robert Harding Picture Library Ltd,
75b Don Johnston, 82 © Robert Harding Picture Library Ltd, 83tr © All
Canada Photos, 83b © SCPhotos, 86tl © blickwinkel, 92b © RGB Ventures
LLC dba SuperStock, 95bl © Animal Imagery, 99t © Purple Pilchards, 99b ©
CRG Photo, 101tl © National Geographic Image Collection, 102tr © National
Geographic Creative

Ardea: 66t © Theo Allofs / Biosphoto, 66br © Philippe Henry / Biosphoto,
86tr © Stefan Meyers

Dreamstime: 6l © Serban Enache

Corbis: 83tl Jenny E. Ross

Getty: fcc Daisy Gilardini, 5tl Suzi Eszterhas/ Minden Pictures, 21 Jerry
Kobalenko, 29 Daniel J. Cox, 33tr David Courtenay, 36tl Daniel J. Cox,
36bl John E Marriott, 36r Joe McDonald, 40tl Mark Newman, 64 Doug
Lindstrand, 65t Jak Wonderly, 65b Doug Lindstrand, 74 Don Johnston,
78t Norbert Rosing, 78b Steven Kazlowski, 79r Wayne
Lynch, 96-97 David & Micha Sheldon, 103 Keren

FLPA: bcc Patrick Kientz/Biosphoto, 2 Mark Raycroft/
Minden Pictures, 4 Jan Vermeer/Minden
Pictures, 5b Patricio Robles Gil/Minden
Pictures, 8 ImageBroker/Imagebroker, 9tl
IMAGEBROKER,CHRISTIAN HÃ¼TTER/
Imagebroker, 9tr ImageBroker/Imagebroker, 9b
David Hosking, 10 IMAGEBROKER,ALFRED
& ANNALIESE T/Imagebroker, 11tr Ingo
Arndt/Minden Pictures, 12t Sumio Harada/
Minden Pictures, 12b Donald M. Jones/
Minden Pictures, 13t Mark Sisson, 13b
Sumio Harada/Minden Pictures, 18-19
Sergey Gorshkov/Minden Pictures, 20tl
Jim Brandenburg/Minden Pictures, 20tr
Jim Brandenburg/Minden Pictures, 20b
Jim Brandenburg/Minden Pictures, 22
Jim Brandenburg/Minden Pictures, 23t
Jim Brandenburg/Minden Pictures, 23bl Jim
Brandenburg/Minden Pictures, 23br Jim Brandenburg/
Minden Pictures, 24tl Sumio Harada/Minden Pictures, 24tr
Sumio Harada/Minden Pictures, 24b Donald M.Jones/Minden Pictures, 25
Donald M.Jones/Minden Pictures, 26-27 Sumio Harada/Minden Pictures, 28t
ImageBroker/Imagebroker, 28bl Sumio Harada/Minden Pictures, 29br Suzi
Eszterhas/Minden Pictures, 30 Tim Fitzharris/Minden Pictures, 31tl Jurgen
& Christine Sohns, 31r Tim Fitzharris/Minden Pictures, 37 Tim Fitzharris/
Minden Pictures, 38 Donald M. Jones/Minden Pictures, 39tl Steve Gettle/
Minden Pictures, 39tr Jim Brandenburg/Minden Pictures, 40b Michael
Quinton/Minden Pictures, 41 Donald M.Jones/Minden Pictures, 42 Jan
Vermeer/Minden Pictures, 43tr Frans Lantin, 43br Otto Plantema/Minden
Pictures, 44l Frans Lantin, 44tr J.-L. Klein and M.-L. Hubert, 45 Fritz Polking,
46 Robert Canis, 47tl Paul Sawe, 47tr Terry Whittake, 47b Andrew Mason,
48t /Imagebroker, 48bl Jan Vermeer/Minden Pictures, 48br Matthias Breiter/
Minden Pictures, 49r Yva Momatiuk & John Eastcott/Minden Pictures, 51bl
Norbert Wu/Minden Pictures, 52t Mitsuaki Iwago/Minden Pictures, 52b Jan
Vermeer/Minden Pictures, 54-55 Hiroya Minakuchi/Minden Pictures, 56tr
Mark Raycroft/Minden Pictures, 60b Yva Momatiuk & John Eastcott/Minden
Pictures, 68tl IMAGEBROKER , MICHAEL KRABS,Imag/Imagebroker, 68tr
Mike Lane, 69 Jurgen & Christine Sohns, 70 Donald M.Jones/Minden Pictures,
71t Mark Newman, 71bl Donald M.Jones/Minden Pictures, 72 Sumio Harada/
Minden Pictures, 73t Sumio Harada/Minden Pictures, 73bl Jules Cox, 73br
Donald M.Jones/Minden Pictures, 76 Yva Momatiuk & John Eastcott/Minden

Pictures, 77tl Yva Momatiuk & John Eastcott/Minden Pictures, 77bl Donald
M.Jones/Minden Pictures, 77r Martin B Withers, 80 Katherine Feng/Minden
Pictures, 81tl Juan-Carlos Munoz/Biosphoto, 81tr Katherine Feng/Globio,
81b Katherine Feng/Globio, 84-85 Rob Reijnen/Minden Pictures, 87l Yossi
Eshbol, 88 Sergey Gorshkov/Minden Pictures, 92t Donald M. Jones/Minden
Pictures, 93 Michael Gore, 94b ImageBroker/Imagebroker, 94-95t Konrad
Wothe/Minden Pictures, 95r F1online/F1online, 98 Terry Whittaker, 104
Cyril Ruoso/Minden Pictures, 105tr Cyril Ruoso/Minden Pictures, 105b Xi
Zhinong/Minden Pictures, 106t IMAGEBROKER,KERSTIN LANGENBERGER/
Imagebroker, 107 J.-L. Klein and M.-L. Hubert, 108 Samuel Blanc/Biosphoto,
109tr Konrad Wothe/Minden Pictures, 109b Norbert Wu/Minden Pictures,
110-111 Tui De Roy/Minden Pictures, 112 Donald M.Jones/Minden Pictures,
113tr Daphne Kinzler, 115tr John Eveson, 119 Yva Momatiuk & John Eastcott/
Minden Pictures

Nature picture Library: 16 © Steven Kazlowski, 17tl © Bengt Lundberg, 17tr
© Steven Kazlowski, 17br © Steven Kazlowski, 44br © DAVID TIPLING, 53
© Doug Allan, 60t © Chadden Hunter, 61 © Onne van der Wal, 89t © Bryan
and Cherry Alexander, 89b © Bryan and Cherry Alexander, 90-91 © Sergey
Gorshkov, 100 © Diane McAllister, 101tr © Yukihiro
Fukuda, 101b © Diane McAllister, 102tl © Yukihiro
Fukuda, 105tl © Florian Möllers, 118b © Wild
Wonders of Europe /Widstr

Shutterstock: fct/bcr PinkPueblo, bct/
throughout debra hughes, 1 FloridaStock,
6tr Zuzule, 7 Vivienstock, 11br Volodymyr
Burdiak, 14-15 David Osborn, 31bl Holly
Kuchera, 58 Namay Dolphin, 59tl CHEN
WS, 59tr Rat007, 59b Kertu, 62-63 Danita
Delmont, 66bl Uliya Krakos, 67 Anna
Kucherova, 68b Michael Wick, 71br
Sergey Petrov, 87 skapuka, 102b treasure
dragon, 106b tryton2011, 113br Bruce
MacQueen, 114 Volodymyr Burdiak,
115tl Bildagentur Zoonar GmbH,
115b Ondrej Prosicky, 116-
117 Volodymyr Burdiak,
118tl Lenkadan,
120 Jarry

Contents

Adélie Penguin

More than two million Adélie penguins live in Antarctica and on its nearby islands. Parents use stones to build their nests, and they both take care of the chicks.

Alaskan Malamute

Fluffy Malamutes are wolflike dogs that pull sleds in the Arctic. Their double coat of fur is super-warm and even the insides of their ears are fluffy! These puppies are full of energy and love to play in the snow.

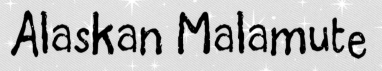

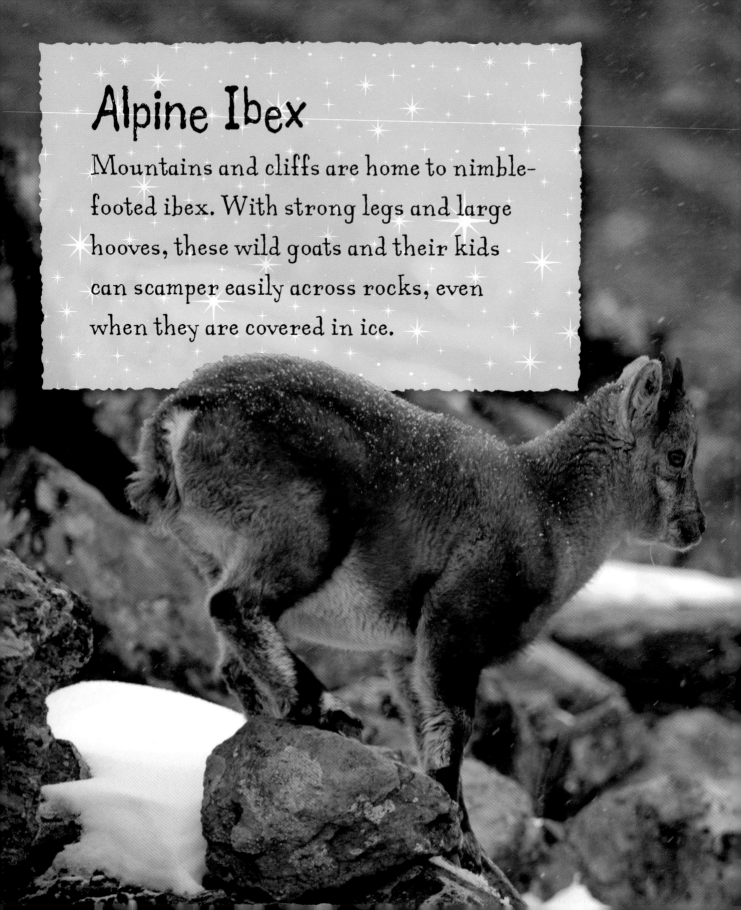

Alpine Ibex

Mountains and cliffs are home to nimble-footed ibex. With strong legs and large hooves, these wild goats and their kids can scamper easily across rocks, even when they are covered in ice.

Alpine Marmot

The Alps are large mountains in Europe, where there is always some snow—even in summer! Moms have their babies in spring, and the family feasts on flowers before the winter snow comes.

American Bison

Winter is coming to an end and the first shoots are starting to poke through the melting snow. This is the time that baby bison are born.

Bison calves walk almost as soon as they are born. They drink their mother's milk, but soon they graze on grass, too. Calves grow fast so they are ready to face the bitter wind and blanket of snow that the next winter will bring.

Arctic Fox

When it is cold outside, Arctic fox
cubs stay cozy inside their burrow.
On warm days, they come out to play!
Arctic foxes grow brown coats in the
summer and white coats in the winter
to help them hide in the snow.

An Arctic fox mom is very busy. She can have two litters of cubs in a year, and often has more than five cubs in each litter! Dad stays with Mom to help her feed and care for their growing family.

Arctic Hare

White Arctic hares can hide from hungry foxes and eagles when there is snow on the ground. A baby hare is gray-brown, and is called a leveret. Its fur turns white in time for its first winter.

Arctic Wolf

The ground is always frozen in Greenland so Arctic wolves can't dig a den for their babies. Cubs are born in cozy caves instead. Soon the cubs are big enough to go outside and explore.

Bighorn Sheep

The Rocky Mountains are home to bighorn sheep. They live in family groups called flocks. Dad has huge horns that can weigh as much as all the other bones in his body put together.

The lambs are amazing because they can walk when they are just a few hours old. Bighorn sheep clamber up steep slopes, stopping to nibble any plant they find. They can even run, jump, and swim!

Black Bear

Cold winds and fluttering flakes of snow don't bother bear cubs! Black bears can cope with almost anything. They live in the wild in Asia and North America.

Bobcat

Like all cats, a bobcat kitten is curious and full of mischief! It loves to climb and chase. When the weather turns cold, the kitten runs back to the tree hole or cave where Mom is waiting.

Brown Bear

Bear babies are very big! They are called cubs. They sleep in dens when it is very cold. Bear cubs like to roll in the snow and explore their forest home.

Snow lays thick on the ground and there is not much food to eat in the winter. This mother bear ate plenty of berries and roots in the summer. She stored up layers of fat under her fur to keep her and her babies warm.

Common Gray Wolf

Playing in the snow is so much fun when you have a thick coat to keep you warm! Gray wolf cubs are clever and cute, but they grow into fearsome hunters.

Coyote

Coyote cubs are cared for by both Mom
and Dad, who bring food back to the den.
They listen for the sound of mice scurrying
beneath the snow
and then pounce!

38

Dall's Sheep

It can be very cold at the top of a mountain, where Dall's sheep live. Sometimes, there is still snow on the mountaintops in the summer. A mother sheep is called a ewe, and her baby is called a lamb. The lamb climbs, runs, and jumps along the rocks.

Emperor Penguin

The Antarctic is the coldest place on Earth. Winter lasts for six months. Life is hard, but millions of penguins make their homes there. Emperor penguin babies are called chicks. They hatch out of their eggs in the middle of winter.

The mother walks to the sea to catch fish. It will be two months before she returns. The father looks after the chick. He holds it on his feet so it doesn't freeze on the ice. The chick is gray and fluffy. When it is summer and time to go swimming, the chick will have its black and white feathers.

Fallow Deer

Little fallow deer fawns are always looking and listening for danger. They move quickly when they are scared. Fawns have brown fur with white spots. When the spring comes, they will hide under bushes or trees.

Gentoo Penguin

Gentoos are noisy birds, squawking and calling to one another. They live in the frozen Antarctic and dive into the sea to catch fish. The chicks hatch from eggs that are laid in nests of stones!

49

Harbor Seal

Harbor seals are playful and enjoy tossing seaweed into the air! A baby seal is called a pup. Harbor seal pups can swim soon after they are born. They stay with Mom until they are about six weeks old.

Harp Seal

Harp seals swim in the icy Arctic Ocean. They have thick layers of fat and fur to keep them warm. Although seals spend much of their lives in the sea, their pups are born on land.

A harp seal pup is born with a thick layer of white fur, and it cannot swim for fish until it has grown a new coat of dark fur. This hungry pup is waiting for its mother to dive into the water and bring back some crabs and fish to eat.

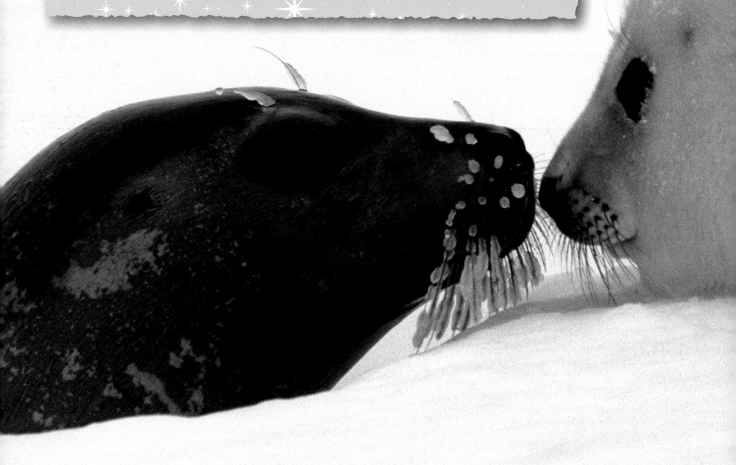

Husky

Huskies are smart and friendly animals. They are fast runners and they love to chase each other in the snow. Huskies are Arctic dogs that live where the winters are very long and ice-cold winds blow. They live in groups called packs and huddle together to keep warm.

Icelandic Horses

Iceland is a small island near the Arctic Ocean
with a long, dark winter. The horses that live
there are small, but tough and smart. The
shaggy hair on their necks is called a mane.

King Penguin

King penguins lay their eggs in the spring and look after their chicks in the summer, when it is still cold and snowy! These water-loving birds live near the South Pole.

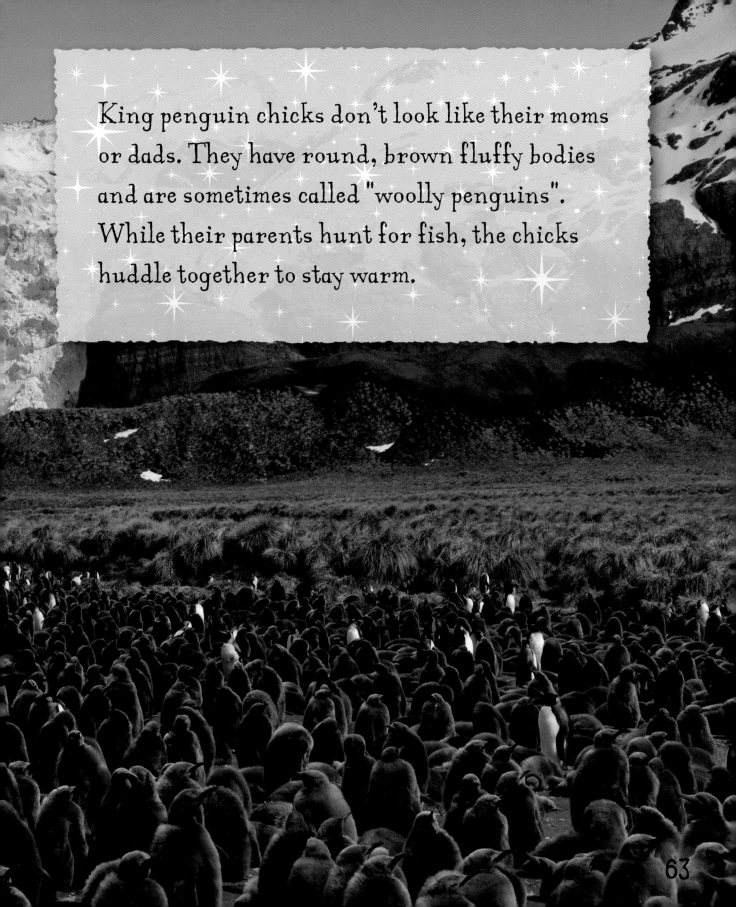

King penguin chicks don't look like their moms or dads. They have round, brown fluffy bodies and are sometimes called "woolly penguins". While their parents hunt for fish, the chicks huddle together to stay warm.

Kodiak Bear

All brown bears are big, but Kodiak bears are the biggest of all! Tiny cubs are born in a den in February. They are almost hairless and blind, so they snuggle together to keep warm until spring comes in May.

Llamas and Alpacas

When a llama is scared it spits and kicks! Llamas and alpacas have soft, silky fur and live in the Andes Mountains of South America. A youngster is called a cria, and it stays with the family herd. Dad protects the herd from coyotes.

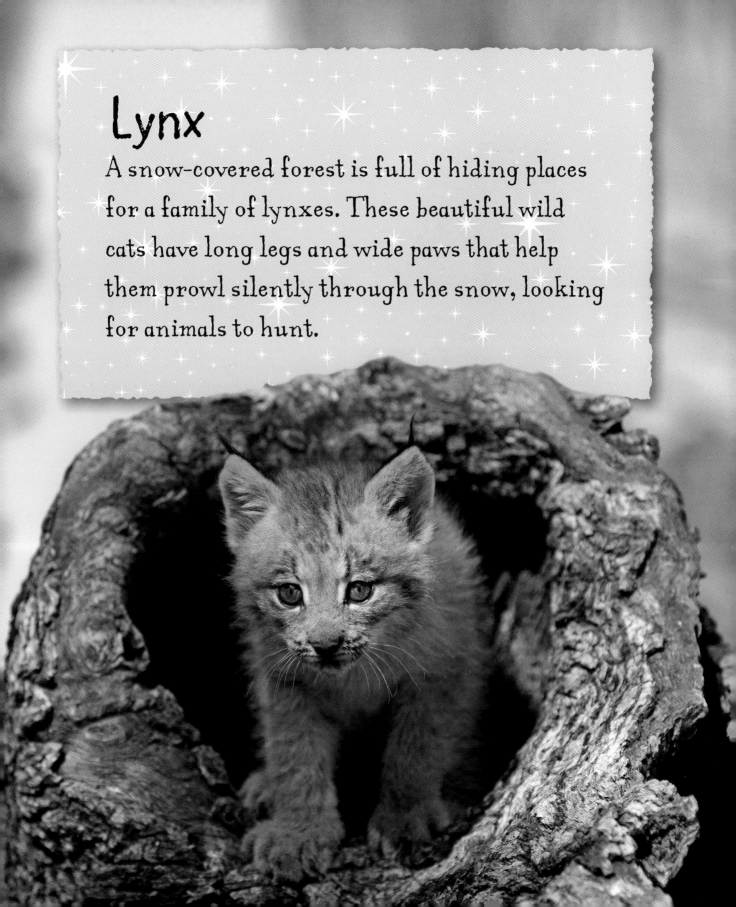

Lynx

A snow-covered forest is full of hiding places for a family of lynxes. These beautiful wild cats have long legs and wide paws that help them prowl silently through the snow, looking for animals to hunt.

Moose

Moose love the cold! If they get too hot they have to sit in a stream to cool down. A young moose is called a calf. Their dads have the largest antlers of any deer.

Mountain Goat

Mountain goats climb up hills and cliffs to hide from bears, wolves, and mountain lions. Even baby goats, known as kids, can skip through the snow without slipping. Mountain goats eat plants and nibble on snow when they are thirsty.

Mountain Lion

The snow is deep, but a cute mountain lion cub doesn't mind! Cubs start to play when they are ten days old. They practice pouncing, chasing, and hiding. Mountain lions are also called pumas.

Mule Deer

A mule deer's big ears twitch and turn to pick up every sound. It is listening for coyotes and mountain lions. At the first sign of danger, deer run away— often jumping high in the air!

Muskox

Muskox families spend the whole year in the Arctic, even during the freezing winter months when there is little grass to eat. The adults take good care of their calves and protect them from wolves and bears.

Panda Bear

A panda bear cub is so tiny when it is born that it weighs the same as an apple. Soon, it is big enough to play outside in the snow. Giant pandas climb trees and eat bamboo.

Polar Bear

Little cubs keep an eye open for danger. When they are bigger, they will be fearless. Polar bears live in the Arctic, and they love the snow. Their fur is so thick that they can get too hot in the summer!

Polar bears are the world's biggest bears. Mom builds her cubs a den, so they are born in a warm, safe place. In the spring, the fluffy cubs come out of the den to explore and learn how to hunt.

Red Fox

Little red fox cubs are often born before the spring sunshine comes. Their mother keeps them snug inside her den while they grow strong. Soon, they can leave their home to play outside. If they get too chilly or wet, they go back inside to warm up.

Reindeer

Little reindeer calves graze on grass just one hour after being born. When they are a day old, they can run faster than a person. Reindeer are also called caribou. They are able to smell grass under a layer of deep snow!

The snow is melting and a calf must eat a lot to grow big and strong. At the end of the summer, it will join its herd on a long journey south to keep out of the worst of the winter weather.

Sea Otter

These sea otter babies love to cuddle
—and so stay close to their mom.
Sometimes sea otters hold hands.
The water is chilly, but sea otters
have the thickest fur of any
animal in the world.

Siberian Tiger

Tigers hunt at night, but in the deep winter they often hunt in the day, too. Little cubs love to play fight, which is a good way to become a great hunter.

94

Mother tigers usually have up to six cubs at a time. The cubs are born blind and helpless. They need their mom to look after them until they are three years old. She will fight other animals to protect them.

Snow Leopard

Very few people have ever seen a snow leopard, and cubs are especially shy. These wild cats live on wintry, windy mountains in Asia. Sleeping snow leopards wrap their tails around themselves like a blanket.

98

Snow Monkey
(Japanese Macaque)

It's a chilly day, but the water is nice and warm! The snow is deep, but a baby monkey can jump into the hot springs nearby if it gets too cold.

Snow monkeys like the snow. The babies even make snowballs just for fun! While the youngsters play, their moms and dads soak in the water to keep warm. Snow monkeys are also called Japanese macaques.

Snub-nosed Monkey

The winters are long and harsh where snub-nosed monkeys live. These little babies don't mind. They have lots of fur to keep them warm. They also get snuggly cuddles from their mom, granny, and aunts!

Walrus

A walrus's white tusks are teeth used to smash ice, or help haul its huge body out of the water. Walruses are big because they are full of fat that keeps out the winter chill. Calves can swim as soon as they are born.

Weddell Seal

It may be summertime in the Antarctic, but there is still snow on the ground and ice floating on the sea. This is the coldest place on Earth. Weddell seal pups are born from spring to summer.

When the sun comes out, a pup basks on the snow. It could swim when it was just two weeks old. Weddell seals dive very deep underwater, hunting for fish. They can stay there for an hour, but they must return to the surface to breathe.

White-tailed Deer

If a white-tailed deer is startled it runs away, flashing its white tail as it goes. Little fawns are born in summer, but they grow quickly so they are strong enough to survive the winter. A mother deer is called a doe.

Wild Boar

All is quiet in the woodland
until a family of wild boar
trots into a clearing.
They squeal and
chirrup to each
other as they snuffle
through the snow,
searching for roots
and worms to eat.

When wild boar piglets are born, they have striped fur which helps them to hide in the forest. Soon they grow thick, dark fur and are brave enough to explore. They also enjoy rolling in the snow!

Wild Pony

Ponies are small horses. They live
on grasslands where they spend
the day grazing on plants
with the rest of the herd.
Baby ponies are called
foals and stay close to Mom.

Horses and ponies grow fur and a long mane to keep their skin dry, even in rain and snow. When they get chilly, ponies gallop around to warm themselves up again!